The Wedding

by Hareem Atif Khan • illustrated by Lesley Danson

Lucy Calkins and Michael Rae-Grant, Series Editors

LETTER-SOUND CORRESPONDENCES

m, t, a, n, s, ss, p, i,
d, g, o, c, k, ck, r, u,
h, b, e, f, ff, l, ll, z, j,
w, y, x, qu, -e, -o, -y,
ch, sh, th, ng

HIGH-FREQUENCY WORDS

is, like, see, the, too, of, says,
to, for, look, you, do

The Wedding
Author: Hareem Atif Khan
Series Editors: Lucy Calkins and Michael Rae-Grant

Heinemann
145 Maplewood Avenue, Suite 300
Portsmouth, NH 03801
www.heinemann.com

Cataloging-in-Publication data is on file with the Library of Congress.

ISBN-13: 978-0-325-13846-6

Design and Production: Dinardo Design LLC, Carole Berg, and Rebecca Anderson

Editors: Anna Cockerille and Jennifer McKenna

Illustrations: Lesley Danson

Photographs: p. 32 (top) © Swapan Photography/Shutterstock; p. 32 (middle) © Digital Cloud/Shutterstock; p. 32 (bottom) © Ali Ashraf Syed/Shutterstock.

Manufacturing: Gerard Clancy

Printed in Dongguan, China
4 5 6 7 8 9 10 TP 28 27 26 25 24 23
April 2023 Printing / PO# 4500868396

Contents

Meet...

Imran

Mom

Yasmin

Taj

Let's Plan!

"Look," says Mom. "A wedding! It will be so much fun!"

"No, it will not," I huff.

"I do NOT like to dress up."

"I do NOT like to sing.

And I do NOT like to dance."

"Hush," Mom says.

"A wedding is the best."

Ding,
dong!

"That must be Taj and Yasmin!"
says Mom. "Go let them in."

"OK, gang," says Taj

"Let's plan for the wedding!"

"I got us lots of fun things!"

"You do henna so well, Taj!"
says Mom.

"Next, let's try a dance!"
says Yasmin.

"No, no, no!" I yelp.

"I will NOT dance."

But Mom says I must.
I hop. I clap. I twist.

I swing my hips.

"See?" says Mom.

"You DO like to dance!"

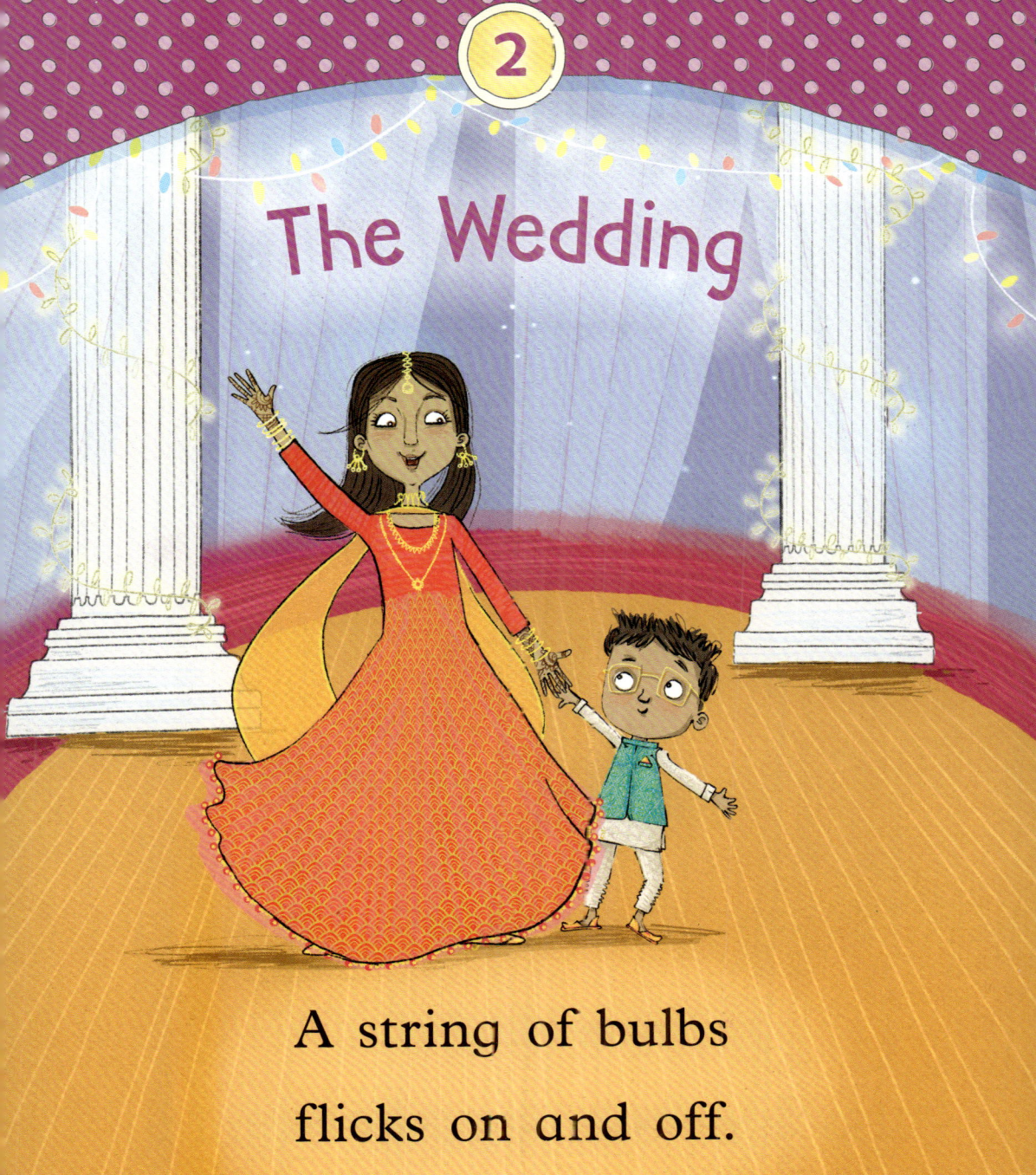

The Wedding

A string of bulbs

flicks on and off.

2

"Look at that!" gasps Yasmin.

"This is the list of songs
we will sing," says Taj.

Mom hits a long, thin drum.

Bup, bup, bud um!

We sing and clap.

Then, we get to see a dance with lamps.

Yasmin and I dance too.

A red rocket zips
up to the sky.

Yasmin tugs on my hand.
"Quick!" she says. "We can't
miss this next bit."

We run to the deck.

"See?" says Mom.

"A wedding IS the best!"

Henna

"Yasmin! Is that henna?"
asks Ms. Ross.
Yasmin nods.

"Yes! My mom did this for me."

"You get henna from a plant,"
Yasmin tells the class.

"You dry the plant, then you crush it and mix it up. It gets wet and thick."

"Then, you put it on
and let it dry."

"I wish I had henna like that,"
says Ms. Ross.

"Me too!" says Tam.

"I can ask my mom
    to bring it in," Yasmin says.
"She is the best at it."

In a bit, Taj brings

henna and snacks.

"My! You can do that
so fast, Taj!" says Ms. Ross.
"Yes, she can!" Yasmin says.

A PAKISTANI WEDDING

Have you ever been to a wedding? At a Pakistani wedding, like the one Imran goes to, people wear fancy, colorful clothes. It can look like a fashion show.

bangles

At a Pakistani wedding, women often wear bracelets called *bangles*. They jingle and clang when you dance, like music! Women also wear jewelry made of real roses and jasmine flowers. It looks pretty, and it smells pretty, like perfume!

Sometimes, men wear a hat called a *turban*. It's made of long layers of cloth, coiled up like a snake.

turban

Some men also wear a curly toed slipper called a *khussa*. Wearing these can make you feel quite royal, like a king.

khussa

Weddings can be fun because you get to wear fancy outfits that you wouldn't wear anywhere else!

Talk about...

Ask your reader some questions like...

- What happened in this book?

- At first, Imran thinks the wedding *won't* be fun. Why does he think that?

- Later, Imran changes his mind and thinks the wedding *is* fun. Why does he change his mind?

- Have you ever been to a big event like a wedding? What did *you* think about it? (If not, would you want to?)